A Suit of Four

A Suit of Four

Poetry by

A. L. Lazarus
Barriss Mills
Felix Stefanile
Bruce Woodford

Introduction by

Constance Hunting

Purdue University Studies
West Lafayette, Indiana
1973

To our students

Acknowledgments

The authors are grateful to the editors and publishers of the following magazines for permission to reprint poems which first appeared in their pages: *Antioch Review, Approach, Beloit Poetry Journal, Carleton Miscellany, Chelsea, The Chicago Tribune, Christian Century, College English, Colorado Quarterly, The Commonweal, Dalhousie Review, Descant, Discourse, Elizabeth, Etc., Galley Sail Review, the goodly co, Hawk and Whippoorwill, The Kansas City Star, Literary Review, Massachusetts Review, Michigan Quarterly, Minnesota Review, The Nation, New Mexico Quarterly, New Republic, The New York Times, Northwest Review, Perspectives, Poetry Broadside, Poetry (Chicago), Prairie Schooner, Quarterly Review of Literature, Quartet, Quicksilver, San Francisco Review, Satire, Saturday Review, Southwest Review, Sparrow, Spokesman, Virginia Quarterly, Western Humanities Review, William & Mary Review,* and *Yankee.*

"Lines from a Poet in Residence" first appeared in *Carleton Miscellany* (Fall 1970).

"Renoir Girl" first appeared in *The Nation* (29 August 1959).

"Escapade" and "Thighbone" first appeared in *New Mexico Quarterly* (Spring 1947).

"Inventio: Crete" first appeared as "Kalispera" in *New Republic* (6 December 1969).

"Spoiled by All My Tyrants" first appeared in *Poetry* (Chicago: March 1955).

"Ripe Olives & Bitter Grapes" first appeared in *Quarterly Review of Literature* (Fall 1967).

"Coffee Jag" first appeared in *Saturday Review* (29 October 1960) as did "Wing and Prayer" (12 November 1960) and "A House Named Sylvia" (30 April 1966).

"The Weather Didn't Do Us Any Good" first appeared in *Virginia Quarterly Review* (Summer 1972).

"Abstract I: Nuns on a Grey Landscape" first appeared in *Western Humanities Review* (Spring 1955).

Introduction

Yet they love their words, these four patient, stubborn poets. They woo their words, they wait them, they measure them, they weight them. And by such various scales, *vide*: Lazarus the quick, the lithe; Mills the contemplative, the delver; Stefanile the compiler, the actuality collector; Woodford the comparativist, the invoker. Different burdens, differing voices; unvarying in their naming and celebration of excellent trophies.

Lazarus is of course no lightweight, swift and decisive as his poems are. Their authority rests in his assimilation and then subsumation of his literary heritage into his own expressive nature. For the particular bent is always his alone. The second poem in his collection begins, "You, Morris Lazarus. . . ." How "You, Andrew Marvell" has been metamorphosed; and the poem is titled "Grandfather." Ancestry doubly acknowledged! Changes continue to be rung, resonances continually set up: in "Chez James," "This was our first residence, / We built it of sticks and stones . . ." perhaps thrown, one parenthesizes. And goes on to read eagerly to the end, wherein the elder child "celebrated her third birthday / the day before we received our transfer notice, / helping us whitewash the pickets / around our strawberry patch." That strawberry patch is a triumph in more ways than one. Read these lines again and listen to the vowels swing along the low-growing strawberry vines, the consonants prickling up like fruit. This is Lazarus' strength: to load his ore with double ore of sound and thought. In

"Friday Afternoons," a poem of football, "I chew the turf with pumping pagan cleats" is somehow risible—we are delighted with it. Why? Because the image and the sound are at one, pumped up with "official" elan and conceit. Technique puns image, sound echoes sense. Who will not enjoy such vintage Cole Porter as "Inebria: Tenerife" with its elided title pun ("In Iberia") and its final mischievous lines: "What are your breakers making?/ Is it only sauterne?" Unlike some wines, Lazarus travels well.

Mills deals in myth, but it is myth with a difference. He does not, here, translate but rather extracts with a knowing contemporary eye and a touch of affectionate deprecation. Here are Venus, the Unicorn, God, Ann Landers, Bach, Renoir, and Sanka. But with that difference: Venus arrives, but "Her land-approach lacks subtlety— / this quattrocento pin-up from the sea." Her waves are "pandering," her thoughts are achieved "through glands," and her last lines are beautiful, as they should be, "this unambiguous girl-gift" who "burns . . . through all cool sufficiencies." The opening lines of "Unicorn" put that fabled beast firmly in its place—"You were never a really popular beast. / Dragon . . . stole the mythical headlines." Not until, again, the last lines does Mills allow his unicorn into "the well-kept garden, / nestling your horned head / (all fierceness lost, / all freedom freely spent) / in a virgin's trembling lap." Mills knows the value of the contrast leading to the right surprise. In other poems, poems of the everyday, one might think, he is able to endow with calm mythic quality the simplest actions and events, as in the monumental "Remembering my Father and the Begonias." How *actual* the action, the watering of house plants; and how the metaphorical motion of the poem enlarges steadily until the final lines that wrench authentically what is best in the human heart:

> Remembering
> now my father and the begonias
> he could love and they, thirsty, silent,
> accept unknowing his silent care.

One of the finest poems in Mills' collection is, in a way, atypical of his more characteristic work, and for the reason that he is listening—and his ear is naturally tuned to the human voice—less than he is looking, because, presumably, he is writing about an artist in the act of painting. "Iola Painting May Apples" deserves to pass directly into our common poetic book. It would not, nor could it, be spoiled by discussion here; but it does not need it, either. It stands quite happily on its own sweet, strong, warm terms.

In general, Lazarus and Mills seem to think poetically in concise phrases no matter how long the single complete line. Stefanile spins a softer, more southerly phrase. Yet the same vision is apparent, the same homage to actuality, to particular things, colored by a sense of unearthly possibilities. Stefanile compiles a litany of many parts: to stone, to names, to tyrants, to victims, to saints, to beaches—a fully orchestrated, brassy, tender, percussive, always musical litany that asks for a full chorus of participants. The poet leaps live from the pit:

> Where is the soul that is free from pride and error?
> We treat truth like a black man in the slums. . . .
> We say Prosperity but we mean Plague:
> the streams and rivers are dying of our wealth,
> the garbage glows like bullion under the sun.

This is from a blockbuster of a poem, an extended modern imitation in a classic mode after the Tenth Satire of Juvenal and familiarly entitled "On the Vanity of Human Wishes." Yet Stefanile can caper, too, as in "How I Changed My Name, Felice": the boy Felice "broke a window like nobody's girl," confesses, his father pays a quarter for his "sin," then "called me inside to look up in a book/ that Felix was American for me/. . .and fanned my little neapolitan ass." Recognition, yes. Part of everybody's experience. "Take from my hand," says Stefanile, "this happy happenstance of herbs and garlands from a ramshackle vale,/ the green and gay plucked from the gray and grim." And don't forget that quite masterful transference of sounds.

From herbs and garlands to "broken glass/purpled in

suns over a barbed land" is but a step. Bruce Woodford's
poems bristle with an exactitude of pain that has its own
stark beauty "like a thorned winter/ white on a tree full
of needles/ aimed every direction." There is the thrift
here which leads to fullness. Not a word is used for any-
thing but meaning. Woodford's intent would seem to be
to make us see his interior landscape in order to make us
feel more keenly our exterior situation. The reverse can
happen, too, as in "Beach Party," where the actual exter-
ior world of the poem becomes interiorized for the
reader by the inclusion of a mythical undercurrent made
explicit in the last stanza:

>   O surely the world must have begun
>   on the seaweed edge in the soft dimpled sand
>   under the light of moon's tugging
>   surely love was the first act
>   after we walked from wave onto the high continent
>   and the first blind living spurt of that tide
>   started in.

Probably Woodford's most ambitious poem is "Running
the Tide," the account of an extended journey south to
Santa Fe, but also the mapping of a spiritual expedition
"down / our own sun-blinded meridian. . . ." The imag-
ery is so packed and yet so accessible to personal and
universal interpretation that what emerges is an Ameri-
can geography of the soul:

>   once they came out of the sea
>   by no map but the unchartered seasons
>   chased each shadowed contour of their dream past
>   waking   wherever day by ridge or river. . .
>   —til fanged bush or drift of sand ground eyes out
>   teeth from weathered jaws and filled the cages
>   of their breath. . . .

This is the route the two contemporaries of the poem
follow by car ("*And if I walked,/ I thought*") through far-
apart towns with names Woodford invests with incanta-
tory magic: San Luis, Garcia, Castilla, Questa, with the
mountains always looming, and finally—"always those
sunlight mountains weighing at our/left shoulder the
Sangre de Cristo leaning. . . ." At the end of the poem

the reader is at one with the travellers, weary, but also with wonder and a spiritual exhilaration.

"Preferences," one of Woodford's poems is titled. But this collection of four contemporary poets does not seek preferential treatment for any one of its distinctive parts. These poets stand each on his own ground. They are not new to poetry; rather, poetry is always new to them. Visitors welcome. Hours to suit.

Constance Hunting
MacDowell Colony
20 January 1973

Contents

A. L. Lazarus

BLESS THIS LAND

Chez James

This was our first residence.
We built it of sticks and stones
at the back of our lot,
trumping the Depression with our own hands.
It was really a double garage,
though all we owned by way of vehicle
was a bicycle with pump.
Loftily
we capped our carport with an A-frame attic.
In the backs of our heads we plotted
that it should someday billet our chauffeur.
Meanwhile it quartered the four of us
in hauteur.
(We filed the babies on the wall bunks.)
The elder celebrated her third birthday
the day before we received our transfer notice,
helping us whitewash the pickets
around our strawberry patch.

Grandfather

You, Morris Lazarus,
Talmud scholar and gentleman's tailor,
denizen of ghettos in London and Boston,
when you finally lectured at Cambridge,
swaying in your exegesis of I-thou,
when you unraveled the threads,
did the divinity students
divine the incredible whole cloth
of your own dénouement?

Poolwise in the San Fernando Valley

We had this pad in Panorama City
overnight a bedroom tract
where thousands of ranch houses jostled
on what used to be one ranch.
From the air you noticed aqua teardrops
weeping in every other back yard.
Gladly we shared our Little Lake Canoga
with a parched family of Lockheed engineers
backed up to our fiberglas panels
ingeniously removable.
We also water-witched a mermaid from Reseda,
glittering cobalt from head to chin
in a scaled ontosaurus swimming-cap
and receding bikinis.
The land across the highway remained unsubdivided,
its sharecroppers sticking indivisibly to their shanty
except when 110 fahrenheit prompted them
to strip down to their flannel drawers
and march across the speedlanes, to our water,
punctuating the crazy progress of the cars
—father, son, grandfather, and great grandfather.
The latter turned out to be a long-distance swimmer
and one of our more durable ornaments.

Elegance in Texas

Fieldstone outside and in,
Tecolote tiles and laminated beams,
this was the house that said
"Impinge, impinge!
Don't hover on the fringe
of things. And let dead lumber
slumber."
Fireplace from tiles to beams,
raised hearth and airborne heart.
Walls of glass framing post oaks
and keenly deep blue skies,
except for cineramic sunsets
and the white Rhode Islands
of unlikely thunderheads.
Overnight rains and morning-after lilies
shooting white between bluebonnets and red brush,
Indian paint-brush firecracking
and jumping the Fourth of July.

A House Named Sylvia

Wallflower by a mossy wall
in the shadow of maple and oak
she had stood too long neglected by swain.
We were going to do her over—or so we thought.
We lifted her face and furnace
scrubbed out her coal-smoked soul
painted sun to her clapboards
and after a fashion becoming to ladies
dusted her shingles blue-white.

But she spat diamonds to the winds
stuck to her zinc hatpin
winked at clouds
made pacts with tornadoes.
To inform our maudlin sunshine
her brown stain bled, and soot drifted from her pores.

Darkly from her chimney she sent signals;
her messages came from the hearth.
Conversant in more than one tongue
though resisting polyglot
she rehearsed us in substitution drills.
At night she ran labs and seminars
leading us mim-mem into restoring
her original weather-warped front tooth.
We learned from her the language of welcoming.

With a clock in each mouth
we smiled at forests.
For Sylvia we went into woods
we never came out of.

Great Lakes Gothic

This was our snowbound saltbox with smokestack,
the snow softening its sober outer posture
and giving the lie to drunken slants within.
Ceilings, walls, and lintels pitched tipsy on heavy seas,
the tilted floors sent us reeling into jigs,
and we bobbed sans benefit of cider,
or stuck together—taffies, tars, and avatars.
The gallery had been added aft; above the anchor
of our yard this cabin rose on wooden pins,
naked as a barge in dry dock.
While our crew broke icicles from snowmen on the
    shore,
First Mate and I banked up around the ribs
to keep the winds from freezing decks and pipes.
But there were warmer moments forward
when, gathered at the window of our bridge,
we watched cake-frosted carriers and men-of-war
float by on chainless bottoms and perilous drifts.

Friday Afternoons

The kickoff is a launch of love; in flight
or flutter the dove is received with ceremon-
ial respect, clasped to this runner's ribcage
like a message from the Holy Ghost.

My loins quicken to a call of trumpets.
As the heavenly bird is snapped to me,
I click from rabbit spurt to centaur gallop;
I chew the turf with pumping pagan cleats.

Making a first down stirs my religion up.
And faithful to my ends, I only err
in strategies. Impolitic at times
toward left or right, I hurl my moment's truth.

Between the halves the warden's locker words
may intercept my visions of an angel
in red sequins, tossing silver excla-
mations in the cold unravished air.

The other team is also an affair
of love; the enemy is zen-inertia,
hollow disengagement from the ground rules,
lack of traction for the yardage leaps.

While padded crowds and hungry scholars munch,
something in me celebrates Good Friday,
says farewell to flesh, cries "Stop the clock!
Oh, let there be only Football Fridays!"

Cards Noses Rings

Informing people whether they exist
(in this old telling game of programed cards)
does anyone prefer punched cards and noses
counted over nostrils pierced for rings?

The universal factories make cards,
the factual universities count noses,
the prestidigitators conjure rings
of ash: "We automate; hence we exist."

But how the garbage of these digital cards
suggests disposal lest the smells persist
without retrieving man from reptile rings
and fish-scale! Should we only hold our noses?

What is humane in any of these cards?
ID or even C r e d i t may not ring
love's bell; it takes spirits of roseblood nose-
gays to revive one's ghost that just exists.

Crown individuals with the radiant ring,
punch uniformity right on the nose,
adore whatever shadow makes sans card
a vita and discovers who he is.

Essay, Man, on Mr. Fountain's Dixie

If what they say about Dixie isn't true
enough, Pete Fountain's statement is a coup
to send collective unconscious back to class
and make New Orleans truly worth a mass.
No need to freeze one's entrails under lock
and stock when Bourbon St. toasts Plymouth Rock.
(Let drummer skip a beat, then double-sock.)
Look away while Peter parses tense and age:
the opus on the piper's lips melts rage;
once conjugated by his clarinet,
the tune explains Antoine to Antoinette;
the palsies of dark knees and knuckles cease
when Pete's heroic coupling with the piece
is made. To paraphrase Yeats' accolade,
we cannot tell the player from the played.
Forget the lovelorn bigots' hunting-horn.
Rejoice! Handclap footstamp religion's born
again. Let fingers snap and knees bend native,
breaking, bruegheling, in a récitative.
Glory be to God right on this sphere:
repeal the scare and repossess the air!

Aubade

Truly, Paris must be worth a mass . . .
From the top of his tree
(Mais oui! Mais whee!)
at the top of his joy
our ramrod boy
our cardinal
sings his head up.
At the drop of a ray
this Gaul greets the day
with a paean for "Paree":
"Paree
Paree
Paree
Paree"
Such liturgy!
Our cardinal sings his red up.

The Rollerdrome

Save in this most American of places
where will you find such happy happy faces?
The key that winds up commisars and kings
turns grandpa young, turns junior's wheels to wings.
The waltzing rexing flexing figure-eighters
keep weaving past the just plain family freighters;
none bends but to the organ's bouncy sound
and no one pushes anyone around.
The buoyant organist will all but pour
himself into the notes of Isham's score,
me-tic-u-lous-ly syn-co-pates Kahn's song
as we serenely skate and scoot along.
"It had to be you," we hum; we had to be free;
nobody but you would do, Miss Liberty?

(*After rereading a poem by Emma Lazarus*)

Local Habitation

Aside from smog, and dry or debauchee,
we breathe a giddy alchemy: the tree's
green blood, the schlachthaus pus, my smokehouse
    sweat,
your photosynthesis. Whatever's foul,
whatever's fair (the apple's bloom, the vinegar's
howl) through lung and gill and maidenhair
is it our will to breathe this air, this stuff
that's stung by yahoo turds and sweetly hung
on hummingbirds, this atmosphere that whets
the winter's sex yet in its heat exhumes
a witch's hex? Where sound is raped by jet
or hushed in holy lock with mountain water
running over rock; this drafty stage,
this flighty space where moths may dance and sau-
cers race, this mammoth crematorium
round which the sky vibrates for everyone
gone up in smoke (first flames and second mates)
—is this our home? While ancient stars implode
is this the bar where novices just fade?
Breathe deep breathe shallow, breathe systole dias-
tole, like gasping fish we're hooked upon
catastrophe. In breathless haste, in mal
de mer, pull what we will from Anywhere,
this ineluctable elixir is all
that's there; and there it is, this island air.

SOME WOMEN

Riddle of the Cage

The woman's bird is caged.
Canary Islander
it gives the saddest squeak
as of a voice unhinged.

Perched on its frozen swing
it only blinks a wing
the way the woman blinks
and cannot mean a thing.

The bird is green and yellow;
the man-made cage is black
and disinherits trills.
It gives the lady chills.

Ripe Olives & Bitter Grapes

"Now sing an even sadder song,"
the disinebriated wino said,
"Let's hear it on your seasonal guitar."

"In Avignon I met a vision of a girl,
an olive-lovely girl,
who harvested her hair
in a honeydew chignon
and on her melon skin she wore
warm whisperings of sin."

"Oh, where has she gone,
my olive-lovely girl,
my girl of Avignon?"

"To the snows, to the snows,
you lost your only love;
you lost her to the cruellest snow of all."

Style

While her inquisitors
hit the ceiling
or stomped upon the floor
Sister Teresa of Avila
somewhat mystical about
the divinity of love
(and in her bare feet
no doubt naive about
the consequences of
anti-gravity)
tuned into one of the
middle wave lengths and
... levitated.

(*After reading* The Eagle and the Dove *by V. Sackville West*)

Carnegie's Kid

Like too many others, perhaps,
up to her knees in boots and
down to her bottom in jeans
yet like nobody else
under cover of paperbacks.
She's the new museum piece
in Andrew's libraries
and not altogether for free.
With her garlic breath she abhors,
to the back of her teeth, our ethic
but not Sir Horace Walpole's gothic.

What else does she like?
Franny & Zooey and Zorba the Greek,
The Magic Mountain over Cross Creek;
though more accomplished in dialects
than dialectic, she fraternizes with
Outsiders and sleeps with Sisyphus.

See what you've done, Andrew Carnegie,
and rejoice!

Girls' Heads* Bent on Taking a Test

Front rows
Bubble-of-maple, Applebutter
Coxcomb, Cobweb
Teal, Oatmeal
Vixen, Flaxen
Silversieve, Blackolive
Maraschinocherry, Gooseberry
Pompomyellow, Marshmallow

Middle rows
Tobaccoboll, Orangeroll, Charcoal
Sienna-clay, Ice-soignée, Straw-soufflé
Copperdipper, Sevenupper, Chilipepper
Honeyball, Taffypull, Waterfall
Nutmeg, Eggnog, Coconut
Cinnamonbark, Meadowlark
Mink-mouton, Pink-cotton

Rear rows
Bird's-nest, Everest
Meringue-caffeine, Tangerine
Peatumber, Wheatamber
Zebrastreak, Mozambique
Croissant, Bonbon
Cider-rain, Champagne
Gingerale, Pigtail

Bouffants in sunbeams from high windows

Unconditional Surrender

Matrons win me with sly food,
patrons with hard cash;
girls on cycles catch my sigh
     if the dizzy wind is high;
but when Andráya takes my hand
     I am undone as flowing sand.

One Ticket, One Dance (Penny Opera)

"Wait," he cried, waltzing his muse around the outer
    fires,
the suburban embers, "are you a singer of songs
    yourself?
Do you compose or just audition?"

                                        She caught her breath
on a flying trumpet: "Why, what have I to do with all
    that jazz?"

"I don't know what or why or where; your looks excite
the sullen air; your body takes such reckless poses—"

"Don't take such liberties in public; a poet should be felt,
not feeling; a poet should be heard, not seen;
a poet should not even mean.
Your ticket says we dance; so just keep dancing, Buster."

"I thought at first that I had breached you;
alas, I haven't even reached you."

"One moment, please, before you leave—
who *are* you? Who, in Hell, do you think you are?"

"I wish I knew," he smiled,
dying again in her embarrassed arms.

Song: Rose Pense

Rose Pense, Rose Pense,
with your flammable name
and your hateful incense,
je pense que je t'aime.

Rose Pense, Rose Pense,
are you thorny or tame,
are you spirit or sense,
am I eaten by flame?

A penny for your thoughts,
Rose Pense, and none for my dame.

Portrait of a Lady from New England

She has that kind of conscience; that is one
possession half possessed by her, half free
to bring her nothing much besides the sun
and make bedrock her stern economy.
She will not look at lack; that's her donnée.
And I, who hunger after goods I want,
must marvel when I see her meet each day
as cool New Hampshire meets serene Vermont.

Parable

The mini
Curtain rises on the
Country of the
Thigh.
Delight fills the
Eye, unthreads one's
Needle, makes
Men
Rich, doesn't do a
Thing
For camels.

TRAVELING

Hydrotherapy at Mandal, Norway

Disarmed by warmth
by the Gulfstream's intemperate hand
up the crescent of her silkiness
this wanton Bay invites my bath
but also my undoing

in the rustling turquoise
I respond   at first a jellyfish
the eye of my belly
scanning the immaculate sands

then gently gently flagellating
I generate some arms and legs
and in slow motion I become
an astronaut slipping side to side
bouncing on the moon

"L'après-midi d'un Faune"
drifts from a radio on the beach
and I am programmed helplessly again
into another order of being.
Dear Lamb of God
not the total metamorphosis
not a ballet-dancing nymph
I touch my genital
to know that it is there
for even at Mandal
the vas deferens can make
as the saying goes
a vast difference

Traveler's Agent

Cradling a swan white telephone
in the curve of her Leda-lovely neck
but bussing the moment's silence mauve
with her country-store placebos and asides
("where there's life there's hope")
she confirms at last my space
in the sullen clabbered sky.
While her sweetcream smile, flush, ripeness
bursting decolleté et ceteris paribus
lure clichés to a thousand deaths,
her "life-hope" oracle sounds right,
suddenly, above the crashes
blackening this morning's paper.
So I must ask:
What hope may an inter-olympian loper,
booked out of this cornfield office,
out of these ice-cream snow mounds,
dispatched to the dairy sky, curd to whey,
entertain if he returns
(according to the myth) alive?

Old Caballero (Barcelona)

Cherish your blemish, old caballero;
polish the pearl of its ravishment.
While sir paragon plays as the seahorse plays
what scars of war or birth or harness,
what unhushable heraldry (oh you short-girthed
congenital armless) drives you beautifully mad
to saddle a swordfish? Aficionado:
is a wry psoriasis driving you out of your skin?
Bridle the bite of your unarmed vision.
To your cleft upper lip give a stiffer lower;
hitch clipt penultimate to a tighter ultimate.
The one-eyed rider is all he survives.
Oh, to hold touch by the reins of the blind!
Has somebody's irony put out your eyes?
Rich fool and foil, you picador of paradise.

Smaller Elephants	Cooler Poems
In the Land	of Kalevala
beyond the Bluffs	of Beowulf
they use pairs of tusks	for tog hooks
on the backs	of bath house doors
so that as you	sit entranced
the rest	of the elephant
like a ton	of recollection
may crash	at any moment
through your	fragile privacy.
It is then	in such a state
of	untranquility
(the uncertainty	of steam—
the not too distant	trumpeting)
you may sweat	the inspiration
that mini	ature elephants
or even Mari	anne's real toads
can sometimes	prove more useful
than a sauna	full of ivory
a sauna	full of gold

Stewardess

Under her wing we lose our fear of heights,
lowing at the skies like troglodytes.
Disaster is the last of several odds
and ends we think about. Her gods, our gods.
And truly a divinity has shaped
this lass. Ever* unravished, capped and draped
for feeding various hungers of the heart,
she keeps her travelers and ennui apart.
Did ever fates contrive by storm or fire
or fuses blown or engines split to wire
such possibilities to kill the mile
as trail her tailing down the endless aisle?
While she performs her Grecian Urn-like rites
what cruel logic ties us to our seats?

Boneless on the Monon

Riding on the Monon in December,
never mind your bones;
let snowy fields glide by,
the breakable glass ponds,
the skaters in molasses,
plaids & pompoms courtesy of Currier & Ives.
Depend upon this team of diesels
to neigh along the rails,   ·
their tow chains clanking,
their sledges swaying,
their tails flying in our faces.
On, Percheron! On, Charger!
Throw away the sleighs—you've got us saddled!
Now we gallop past the silos, corn cribs,
hogs magnificent in mufti,
and on high stilts the formal water
blessing out the towns of Battleground
and Chalmers, Rennsselaer and Hammond.
We must hoot at V-8 horses stalled
at crossings, buried in snow sidings. . .
Near the Windy City (past sticks
and stones?) if wind whips up harsh names
it will not harm our bones:
Anaesthetic with an old narcotic
all equestrians pull boneless
into Dearborn and Van Buren.

Letters From Three Islands (Inventio, Inertia, Inebria)

1. *Inventio: Crete*

On Crete one night at the Palace Theatre,
anti-climax to more genuine ruins,
I saw a Bondish movie with Mycénean titles
in which the lovely Hellene spy, after fruitless
encounters with the agent, finally offers
herself (flash/flesh) like a bowl of muscats.
Whereupon out of the winedark audience
on holiday from marble breasts,
one native goatboy spouts a Dionysian "Ha-ha?"
laughing all the way out of the Minoan columns,
all the way down the agora,
pan into the topless evening, the kalispera.

What laughter! What discovery!
What scorn for censors who'd only allow
a grapefly peep at cineflesh!
At first his ha-ha's stung the air
like gouts from the interrogative Aegean.
Then they settled down and sailed,
gulls on the updraft, crying epithets,
crying Málista! Endáksi! Paracaló!
Please—show loveliness as it is!
Eycharistó! Thanks for naked skies!

2. *Inertia: La Palma*

On the Island of La Palma
in the faraway Canaries
the ocean whispers to volcanoes
the lava talks right back to the waves
mountain and sea in a tilt of love.

Half deaf to roosters' early calls
one rises later than the sun
to smells of crab and coffee roast
from shore and quay and Gran Mercado.

After swimming and siesta one can sip
cognac or cola at a hillside dulceria,
watch cobalt-turquoise water mix
with purple down the palette of the bay,
note lichen tame the fire of tiles
on roofs among the lemon groves,
count green-banana frescoes
up the foothills to the clouds.

On the Island of La Palma
lyrics float on lazy air.
The children chirp, the parents sing,
the dark young god of honing
blows his soft-sell pipes of Pan:
"Anyone for sharper knives?"
But the carvers and the shapers
lie asleep with New Atlantis;
our deadlines wait upon mañana
along with terrible volcanoes.

3. Inebria: Tenerife

What is this ocean saying?
Is it saying "part" and "part"?
What are these breakers breaking?
Are they splitting one's heart?

Puerto de la Cruz . . .
your swells hold something back
of how to gain or lose
—not stretching the rack.

Cavalier over moss-covered rocks,
you smash your glass of white wine,
champagne of salty green blood:
"To cactus and vine!"

These rocks: are you cleaving or slaking?
Are you saying "unlearn, unlearn"?
What are your breakers making?
Is it only sauterne?

Barriss Mills

Venus Arriving

Her land-approach lacks subtlety—
this quattrocento pin-up from the sea.
Clearly she knows who she is
and what she has come for. She's Eve
confronting Adam with contingencies
beyond his tutelage. Borderings
of shell, porpoises, pandering waves
cannot distract from the eye-catching
center. She binds attention
with a coy gesture.

No one suspects her of having
thought, except with glands.
Yet her posturings are no less incisive
for that. She pleads love's awkwardness
and disarray—snake of blown curl,
knees bent in lying submission.
She burns, this unambiguous girl-gift,
through all cool sufficiencies.

Fables

The Greeks tell an old story
of a mother whose twin sons
harnessed themselves to the donkey-cart
and pulled her to town for the festival
when their donkey died.

The townsmen marvelled
at such filial devotion,
and the mother called on the gods
to give them the greatest blessing
possible for mortals. Immediately
they fell down dead.

It's a lovely parable,
full of wisdom and wonder
at the curious fitness of things.
The Greeks understood what life is
and what death is for.

And there's another tale
of the man who asked the gods
for eternal life, but neglected
to specify he was never
to grow old.

The years unstrung his limbs
and took his teeth and eyes,
till life was a ghastly glimmer
in the remnants of a man.

Then even the gods could bear
the sight of him no longer,
and they let him die.

Remembering my Father and the Begonias

Remembering my father and the begonias
he filled the house with.
                              From tiny leaves
and cupped flowers to veined elephants' ears
ranged in pots on tables, windowsills,
sideboard and baby grand.
                              Everywhere
you went in the house were begonias,
seeming to have filtered sun from windows
as long as we could remember.
                              Pitcher
in hand, he moved from room to room
while we watched or didn't watch—
it was only father, watering
the begonias.
                 And more often
in those morning hours alone
in the cold house as heat stirred
in the pipes and light came slowly
at the windows and the boredom
of the office (and the figures
he ranked in columns in his strong,
old-fashioned hand and totted
with the deftness of contempt
for the surrogates they were)
still hung far off.
                    Moving now
among the crisp white plants
in the sunroom as the sun
cleared the trees—pitcher always in hand,
feeding the fleshy plants that grew
slowly and silently, as he grew old
and sick and silent too (or, since
he never moved but in a kind of silence,
silently ceased to move).
                          Remembering
now my father and the begonias
he could love and they, thirsty, silent,
accept unknowing his silent care.

The Husband Pigeon

The husband pigeon with mole-
colored hood and dubious wings
hovers the nest in a gable
of the centenarian house.

Clinging with fanning tail
to the peeling fretwork, he assaults
his mate with male insistence.

Spurned, he stalks with rumpled dignity
across the roof, pecking the air,
gobbling in a pompous rage,
flashing a baleful eye.

Hurt, hurt. His maleness
superfluous to the ancient
ritual in the nest, but caught
in the orbit of these mysteries.

Resigned at last on the ridgepole
he listens with tilted head
to his peeping rivals.

A Poem for the Occasion

When I think of William Carlos Williams
I remember an old bluejay
scolding a cat from his nest
in the eaves-trough over our kitchen window.
That cat was up to no good,
and the jay was telling the whole world
about it. The cat went away,
trying to look as though he'd happened
to be passing through. I never saw
the birds from that nest, to recognize them,
but we've had a lot of bluejays
around here since. And the woods
are full of poets the Old Man
helped hatch and keep the cats away from
till they could do their own scolding.

Chinese Tigers

Chinese tigers
are not to be trusted.

Chinese birds
are non-interventionists,
keeping their places in the landscape
(although the feng huang's
appearance presages social harmony).

Chinese butterflies
(and dragonflies and wasps)
perform their function gaily
as flying bits of shape and color.

Deer and horses
and hens and tortoises
(the turtle, old cuckold,
is unmentionable)
accept their roles with decorum.

The carp, fierce
and beautiful, leaping
the waterfalls, threatens
to turn into a dragon.
But Chinese dragons, unlike
our Western variety, don't
slaver over undraped maidens.
They retire to mountaintops
of contemplation.

The Chinese unicorn,
they say, won't tread
on insects, and appears
only to emperors and citizens
of exemplary character.

But Chinese tigers
can't be trusted. The most civilized
scholar and official, bearing
millenia of restraint
on his dignified shoulders,
may feel the ancient tiger
(from before Confucius
and Buddha and the Way,
and courts and painting
and poetry) pacing,
unappeasable, the forests
and mountains and wild places
of his Chinese soul.

Renoir Girl

Breasts high and open, with
the curving belly, to the sun—
legs and arms nervelessly
sprawled on the knoll.

Eyelids lightly closed,
lips relaxed in enigmatic smiling
at whatever daydream itches
slowly in her mind.

It doesn't matter that the frame
couples her with desultory clouds,
a frond of bush curving
above the round thigh like a never
quite caressing hand.

No touch can break
the budding flesh's perpetual
summer, nor wake
death from this sunshiny dream.

Unicorn

You were never a really
popular beast. Dragon,
breathing fire and gorging
on maidens (impervious
to all but the hard swords
of strong-meat-eating heroes)
stole the mythical headlines.

Frightenable by a thought,
you fled before crass passions
like a woodland ghost.
Rumors of vanquishment
of dragons are unconfirmed.
You skewered no known monsters
on that delicate horn.

Hunters, crossing your spoor
with dogs, soon gave up
the chase, or turned aside
after the deer and the boar—
something to get their lances
into. Only monks and poets
tracked you with words.

Church and bestiaries
theologized your white
impalpability to Christ
(and the Holy Ghost, riding
in your prong). Heralds
stuffed and mounted you
in a thousand coats of arms.

And prying naturalists
abolished you altogether.
But you escaped to forests
of imagination, to frisk
elusive and ambiguous—
a Houyhnhnm, bearing
the Yahoo badge on your brow.

There you still submit
to gentle capture in
the well-kept garden,
nestling your horned head
(all fierceness lost,
all freedom freely spent)
in a virgin's trembling lap.

Mountain Country

I should have been born in a mountain country
where there is always fighting.
A small country, harried by wars,
where you carry a rifle and a knife
and watch each rock and tree
to see if it will move. A country
where your closest friend may suddenly
betray you. Where death walks with you
in the passes.

          I am tired
of this soft country where the days
slide easily in grooves
and we wait for something to happen.
Where no man is an enemy
or a friend. We wear perpetual
smiles, to hide our indifference.
And the children are not happy,
and the old men grumble all day,
and the sun is mild, and the enemy
never comes.

          In that other country
men live and die, defying
the gods. The women wait
for the men at night, and watch them
go in the morning. And the sun
rises, hot and red,
out of the trees in the mountains.

Coffee Jag

I drink too much coffee
and smoke too many cigarettes.
We tried Sanka, but it's not
the same. It's coffee keeps me
alive—the stronger and more of it
the better.

     I drink it hot
and black in a tall green cup
that keeps it from cooling off
too fast. I buy it in three-pound
sacks at the A & P. It smells
great, coming home in the car.
I cook it in an aluminum thing
shaped like an hour-glass. Whenever
it runs dry, I fill it up again.

Right now, it's two a.m.
going on three, and I can't sleep,
and I ought to be writing letters
or checks or doing something useful.
But I'd rather write this poem
in praise of coffee, hot and black
from the pot, and cigarettes.
That's worth being alive for, even
at two a.m. going on three.

A Letter to Ann Landers

There was a time when the world's woes
were addressed to the gods. If Zeus
wouldn't listen, Aphrodite
might. Or one of the lesser gods
intercede with the Olympians.
Now we write to you, Ann Landers.

Your tribunal is attainable
and free. Answers come back
by return mail, or are printed
in your columns, for everyone to see.
Our loneliness and self-pity
are apotheosized.

Reading your column, we forget
missiles poised, brush-fire wars,
the palavering of statesmen. Here
are troubles we can understand:
straying husbands, termagant wives,
wallflowers of either sex.

And drunkenness, money-problems,
small violence, indifference,
and fear, and love. It's love,
trying hard to stay alive
in a quarrelsome world, we want
to tell you about, Ann Landers.

Bach Cantata

How shall I continue sullen,
listening to this song of praise?
As the solemn hallelujahs rise
from the groundwork of counterpoint,
something I had forgotten rises
about me in this room.
The words praise the Lutheran God,
but the music is praise of song
itself—of the joy we do
our daily utmost to deny.
Praise of what man has been
and may become again
in moments when this music
(or spring bursting outside
these windows) filters through
our joylessness.

My Aching Back

Antedating Adam's offense,
the primal affront to gravity—
man's shaking earth from fingertips
to stiffen like a walking tree.

A simple calculation of stresses
confirms man's sin against the spine:
pointing himself, a forked stick,
against the sky and teetering
with each undulation of earth's crust.
The dinosaurs tried it. The great apes
compromised, rising and reaching
but retaining their foursquare grasp
on the planet.

        Grant the marvel of it
and admit we perform surprisingly
well our tightrope walk between
earth and air. Yet we must pay
for making acrobatical history.
Not the Fall, but that upstart Rise
is visited upon me now.

Gone Forever

Halfway through shaving, it came—
the word for a poem.
I should have scribbled it
on the mirror with a soapy finger,
or shouted it to my wife
in the kitchen, or muttered it
to myself till it ran in my head
like a tune.

But now it's gone with the whiskers
down the drain. Gone forever,
like the girls I never kissed,
and the places I never visited—
the lost lives I never lived.

Briefcase

My old briefcase was leaking
papers and poems whenever
I walked to the office and back.
I'd stitched the corners until
they couldn't be stitched any more,
and taped them until no tapes
would stick to them. There was only
one slot that would hold anything
smaller than a Russian novel.

I used to tighten up the straps
and pinch everything to the middle
like a fat man tucking in his shirt.
But it wasn't any use. I'd lose
the notes for my lectures on the way
to class, and my poems were blowing
all over the neighborhood, like leaves.

My wife got me another one—
shiny brown and stiff and new
and strong enough to beat a horse with.
Now I carry my books and papers
serenely as a broker's clerk
with his stocks and bonds. But I miss
the old thing—stained black in places
and brown in others, and colorless
where the leather had worn down
to a paper thinness.

              I remember
the day my father bought it for me
when I first became a teacher—
new and empty and unscratched
as that briefcase, long ago.

At the Jeweler's

Stopping at the jeweler's
to pick up my watch, I wait
while he tests it on a machine
that amplifies its heart-beat
so that we both can listen.

Now the room is filled
with the frail, irregular
ticking that climbs the minutes
like broken waves. The silence
between is weighty, ominous.
Each timid, halting beat
overcomes its heaviness
to utter a small declaration
of energy and sound.

The silence is a monotone,
sure of itself and waiting.
The watch ticks erratically—
overloud and then subdued
and hesitant. A thumb's pressure
or small blow could stop it.

But it doesn't stop, and the silence
is more loudly broken as he says
"She seems to run" and shuts off
the machine. And as I fasten
this second pulse to my own,
we no longer hear its ticking
or the silence (waiting, sure)
underneath the life-beats.

Everybody Cried at our Wedding

Everybody cried at our wedding,
except me. (And the minister,
of course.) My wife cried,
her mother and father and brothers cried,
and there wasn't a dry eye
on my side of the family.
They behaved like a wake
instead of a wedding. The minister
looked up once to make sure
he was reading the right service.
He glanced at me and almost
smiled. As for me,
I was feeling fine, and never
have been able to figure out
what all the weeping was for.
My wife (if she knows, and she
probably does) won't tell me.

Nebuchadnezzar

Nebuchadnezzar, king of kings,
ran naked and four-footed among
the beasts. His body sprouted fur.
Feet and hands turned horny
against the stones. Nettles
clotted his beard and hair.

The courtiers said "O King,
live forever, but return
to your kingdom, your palaces,
your queens and concubines!"
Nebuchadnezzar nibbled grass
and pissed on a stone.

The Garbagemen

As they ride the humpbacked truck
down our street this fine spring morning
(clinging like boys to the handholds
and jumping down with a hop
and short run before the vehicle
grinds to a stop) they shout
"Good morning" and bang the lids
back on the garbagecans
before I've a chance to answer them.

They're limited conversationalists.
There's no chance for repartee
or philosophical remarks
on the weather and such things.
It's not so much a conversation
as a monolog of greetings
to the morning world. They shout
their news on the run. It's only
a quick "Good morning" and clapping
the lids on the garbagecans.

I sometimes think I'll try
to arrest their headlong progress
between the curbs. I might say
"Judging by this morning's leavings,
would you say we're a happy people
in this town? Is the day's collection
of old clothes and broken boxes
a cheerful one? Are people
joyfully ridding their attics
and refrigerators—preparing
for a new life, a new spring,
a new accumulation?"

I might say "This morning in spring—
so hopeful and beautiful—
has it reached into men's closets
and their souls?" But I never say
any of these things. It's only
a loud "Good morning" on the run,
punctuated rhetorically
with the banging of the garbagecans.

Walking North

Walking north, assaulted
by winds like small knives
out of Canada. My cap
and my father's greatcoat
give shelter, but we wear
our faces naked to the weather.

Walking long enough, a man
(as Emerson says) might freeze
like an apple. The heart
is a rare furnace, but cold
steals from it continually.

Meridional alleys, the lees
of houses break, for a moment,
the bitter scything, but my way
swings north again.

And I envy trees, whose hearts
go underground in winter.
Their skeletons stand like husks
till spring unbanks groundfires
and roots pump blood again
through bole and branch and leaf.

While I am peripatetic
and exposed, walking north
through harsh weather.

La Grande Jatte

No Sunday, anywhere,
was quite like this.
No sunlight, ever,
quite so luminous,
or grassy place so inviting,
or trees so well behaved.

No summer city folk,
escaping the boulevards
with children, pets, and parasols,
attain to such repose
in any landscape.

Yet here they stand,
sit, stroll, or fish
with the eternal optimism
and patience of city folk
in the presence of rivers.

Here the tall woman
and her child in white
advance forever along
the long, sunlit embankment.

The upholstered lady with the monkey
dominates by her elegance,
while her escort, half-hidden,
asserts himself with cane
and insouciant cigar.

A black-tophatted gentleman
watches the river, and
the sprawled workman with his pipe
dissociates himself and claims
a share of Sunday for the poor.

How many Sunday afternoons,
how many sunlights on the grass
and boats tacking on the river
and trees marching with the river
and strollers and loungers

gave themselves unknowing
to Seurat's shaping and placing
till his final, tiny
brush-stroke pinned them all
to La Grande Jatte and this
perpetual Sunday of the mind?

Chrysanthemums

Summer is gone.
The other flowers are gone
and winter is almost here.
You hold it back awhile
with your late blossoming.

Frost has turned the garden brown.
It is withering back to earth.
And trees throw up their bare arms
to a cold sky. But you blossom
still, while the last leaves fall
and the last wind from the south
brings in the dying sun.

Once it was summer and violets
and roses I loved. And then
the sturdy tulips and daffodils.
They were brave, the daffodils
and tulips, bringing the sun
before the sun. But you
are braver, my chrysanthemums,
gold and yellow and bronze
and purple and red.

You hold winter back awhile.
You hold back the wind and the cold—
trembling of trees, the dark nights,
the dying sun. Your late blossoming,
your tough greenness and red
and yellow hardihood
hold death back awhile.

Iola Painting May Apples

Under the thin shade
of spring trees, you paint
the may apples. A tall oak
spreads its pale leaves above
the campstool where you sit
in your orange skirt, surrounded
by watercolor gear.

The umbrella leaves
of the may apples cover the ground
with a low canopy. Young trees,
supple and straight, divide
the middle ground vertically.
Behind them an old maple sprawls,
and a tangle of woods.

Roundabout are noises
of solitude—insects buzzing
and flying, a bird uttering
a sharp, metallic chirr.
Far off, a tractor gasps
its slow way around a field,
plowing or planting. The wind
occasionally stirs the leaves.
Sun filters warmly among them.

The shady circle where you sit
is cooler, remoter. My ears
follow a car going by
on the road below. I watch
two black butterflies foraging
among the violets. A tiny spider
climbs the red thermos bottle
beside my book. But you
confront the may apples.

A flicker whinnies, but you
do not hear it. The sunlight
twitching the corner of your painting board
is an annoyance. I shall not
break silence, or offer you coffee
till you've finished with the may apples,
flowing in green pools across the ground,
and the dark trees sectioning
your paper, and the vague woods beyond.

Wing and Prayer

Four years in the Pacific
in the Navy in War Two
and he never quite got over
the seasickness. It wasn't
just the big swells and choppy seas
that set it off again. He
.could feel it even when the water
flowed and folded upon itself
like glass, as regular as breathing.

Then there was Guynemer,
the French ace in that other war,
who said he never learned to fly
without thinking quite deliberately
"Stick left, left rudder,"
banking for a turn. That made him
a successful killer instead
of a sitting duck for anyone
who got behind him and solved
the pattern of his reflexes.

I'd call him a kind of poet,
for poets, too, must keep
their responses fresh, their gestures deliberate.

But let's not forget my seasick friend.
A poem is willed and contrived,
yet no poet ever quite gets over
the vertigo of being alive.

In Memoriam: J.H.W.

Death takes strong-legged men,
asking no questions, answering none.

But no one thought of death, there
where boys' games and boys' things
filled the short winter afternoons
with guns, snares, tracks in the snow.

Or the long summers, with school
far off and the woods near
and large enough for running—
just running, not going anywhere.

He ran (and swung far out
on grapevines, and climbed trees)
because the young, strong legs
wanted to know how strong they were.

Death would have had to run
far and fast to catch him then.

Later, going to college,
working and marrying, the legs
still sometimes wanted to run,
but the woods were smaller then
and farther away.

And if he dreamed of going
somewhere (or getting away
somewhere) the dreams faded
and the circuit closed, from home
to office and back again.

Death didn't even have to follow
to catch him then. Death waited
quietly, while one day's round
turned back upon the day before.

And casually tripped up the middle-
aging legs, and took him.

Brother Mouse

It caught him—spang
behind the ear, as a mouse trap
should. But he struggled
a moment before he died.

I dropped him, trap and all,
in the garbage and set another
for country cousins who might thread
the holes in our old house.

And being no St. Francis,
I serve notice on all mice
and other interlopers that
our house belongs to us.

But still I hate to remember
how he died, fighting for breath
that couldn't come—so great a pain
in so small a creature.

Child's Drawing

Here is our house, all roof
and door and windows. Smoke curls
from an oddly angled chimney.
Grass grows in straight strokes
and a child's bike
leans against a tree.

At the top of the page,
between the prickly sun
and lump of cloud,
is a smaller replica
of house and grass and tree.
Here is God's house and (leaning
against His tree) God's bicycle.

After Winter

On this virginal May morning
after the rain
I forgive my enemies
and my friends and even myself
our mutual sins. The morning
is at peace with itself (young leaves,
the pink redbud, an angleworm
sprawling across the sidewalk).
The birds are yelling at the sun,
newly risen. A million waterdrops
glisten on the grass. Earth is bathed
in gentleness, and all outdoors
has forgotten winter. We cannot
forget. And as I walk
toward the usual day, I feel
death's tug, and winters gone
and to come. But for this moment
it's the birds, the grass, the trees,
drunk on last night's rain, and leaves
and blossoms, unremembering,
unforeseeing, and this fresh
May morning and forgiveness
for us all.

Felix Stefanile

How I Changed My Name, Felice

In Italy a man's name, here a woman's,
transliterated so I went to school
for seven years, and no one told me different.
The teachers hardly cared, and in the class
Italian boys who knew me said Felice,
although outside they called me *feh-LEE-tchay*.

I might have lived, my noun so neutralized,
another seven years, except one day
I broke a window like nobody's girl,
and the old lady called a cop, whose sass
was wonderful when all the neighbors smiled
and said that there was no boy named Felice.
And then it was it came on me, my shame,
and I stepped up, and told him, and he grinned.

My father paid a quarter for my sin,
called me inside to look up in a book
that Felix was American for me.
A Roman name, I read. And what he said
was that no Roman broke a widow's glass,
and fanned my little neopolitan ass.

Stone

Amphitheater of spines
always the stone:
rasp, bevel and bruise of a slum—
the scrape underfoot
the cold echo
drama of heels
rorschach left by rain on porous walls
hard mirror
sun-deceiver stone

to bounce a ball
to scrawl
to lean, and even
on cross evenings, to love:
soft shoulder hard life

stone of worship
veritable jut of Mammon
windows like David-shields in the sun
Ozymandias stone

fort and ruby
spied in the gull's eye
the tanker's earnest garage
pock on the map for aviators
angels
marvel of Martians
lust of advertisers
profit of electric companies

stone friends: the window-washer
the helicopter
the broken sparrow
the gargoyle
the cleaning woman
the surveyor
the abstract artist

blind lens
olfactory stone:
>   the clean harsh of new cement
>   the tic of spoiled neon
>   the right smell of mechanic's grease
>   the long talk of the wind on gasoline
>   wings

all-powerful stone
mood
massif
prop of epochs—stronger than butterflies
>   taller than midgets
>   heavier than go-go girls
>   as expensive as dream
>   as exact as skin

Round of stone—as smooth as the first skull of
>   Testament
Sea of stone—to sail a stony dream
Miracle of stone—Walden into warren
>   men into rabbits
>   befitting to pigeons and their white
>   filth
>   convenient to dogs and cats
>   cannot fool the ant

Stone   stone   stone
that unlike Peter
stays
and stays the heart:
and I the weed to crack the façade
the baroque truant
muddied over with flesh
to fiction your function
with my remembering
of my hometown:

that is a whistle at midnight—
stony moon—
and a sun the color of beer.

That is a sea-gull, scattering sparrows;
that is a young girl
with breasts the size of costume-jewelry ear-rings,
eyes bigger than egg-plants.
That is me:

a street owned by the aura of roasting coffee-beans,
bullied by a newsvendor with a cataract in his left eye
and a hole in his right shoe.
It is charted by social workers with black notebooks and
    flat heels.
Its tourist is the mailman,
bag slung over his left shoulder,
pretzel in his right hand.
It is reminded of its propriety by a nun wearing rimless
    glasses.
It is awakened at dawn by nickelodeons, detectives,
pedlars, pigeons,
and one small boy with a patch in his pants near the
    behind.
They all ring my bell.

Junk-yard and Troy, hometown,
how the wedding goes and the death,
opera and tenor I am your news:
                    counting your bath-tubs whiter than
                        magazines
                    tasting your figs grown in the brick
                    assuring you schedules and
                      delicatessens
                    children quicker than pennies
                    folklore of money and murder
                    pendulous stomachs
                    Sundays of precision—

              starlings,
                  Church,
                      then company:
all the black dresses,
all the new babies,
the assignations.
The piety makes me tremble.

I would make a song out of the ripple of a house-dress,
out of stubs of twisted cigars that smell like wine,
the dank darkness of a tavern,
the round face of lettuce,
crop and rubble of history.

I would make an oratorio of your census
and hymns of good food and hard work for your lesson:
the steadiness of your hatreds
the rot of your rivers
the innocence of your ignorant old ladies
the wisdom of your schizophrenic children
who laugh in two worlds:
the Kingdom of the home, the Republic of the slum.

I appeal to the snobbery of your overalls
the silver of your hammers
the grapes in your blood
the sanctimonies of your rented rooms

O my grouchy, dignified fathers!
I will do all this
who want the gold watch of the sun
                a health or two of remembrance of you
                a little million of love
                for my pound of flesh   my ton of pride.

                and I will write it in stone.

The Weather Didn't Do Us Any Good

The weather didn't do us any good
that famous winter, by the famous sea:
it snowed and snowed. We lived in Noah's city,
or so it seemed—snow was a head-line word,
a terrible miracle. We wished for rain
to wash away the world, and make an end.

It never rained. It snowed, and without end,
the air a fog of ermine, and what good—
even the children sang a song for rain
and the gulls sang their words back from the sea.
The wind laughed outright, carrying a word,
and the snow fell, like ashes, on the city.

We moved like mourners, over the buried city,
through dirtied paths, in queues, joined end to end
by this new discipline of need, each word
a muttered pass-word for some common good:
we might have been mere slaves, a human sea,
locked in emergency. Without the rain

our clever tools were useless, and such rain
as fell turned ice, turned steel. The stricken city
shone icily, a coursing diamond-sea
of peaks and billows, pretty to no end,
where rainbows bared their sabre-teeth. No good
came from the tricky light. The neon word

our beacon flashed was still the same old word.
We read, but never said. Then came the rain,
and washed away the blindness. It was good
to hear the gutters humming through the city,
and watch the snowmen come to a bad end,
and feel the city rising, like the sea,

and shake itself, and shudder, like the sea.
If it was flood we'd suffered through, no word
was written on a wall to tell the end
of anything, because we have this rain,
as steady as the snow, to cleanse a city
not ready for such miracles as do good

when they do good, not bad, to sea or city,
whatever word, like rain, to make an end.

The Day We Danced the Saint

The day we danced the Saint our shoulders worked
beneath the logs, to the music of a march,
and rowdy with religion we cut loose
to try a jig with that long weight on us,
left flank together, then to the right, then left,
running a little, suddenly stopping dead:
the young girls screamed to watch our statue leap
out of its chocks, it seemed, and lean at them,
his fresh paint flashing in the sun like fire.
The band played *Stella Alpina*, and we danced.
red-faced and grinning; grandmothers cackled back
clutching at their black shawls, and throwing sweets
wide of the mark, crunched beneath our feet.
Where we pushed on small children ran with us,
skipping and hopping, calling a father's name,
Papa Antonio!, like that, in public proof
he held his post beneath the logs that bore
our plaster Saint upon the wooden stage,
where dollars gleamed like sequins on his robe
and made a noise like feathers on the wind.
Next to me Rodolfo puffed and swore,
his face damp with religion and its work,
while up ahead fat Father Ferdinand
swung with the weight, the Pope's own pachyderm,
"*Laetantur coeli!*" roaring, to our jibes.
"Don't get to heaven too soon!" Rodolfo cried,
and the logs rumbled, but our Saint stayed put.

I glimpsed my mother, peering through the crush,
torn between love of Christ, love of her son,
whose skinny shoulders she feared surely would crack
beneath that holy rubble overhead,
but I straightened up, and winked, like some famous
    athlete,
along with big Arnaldo, Menechin,
Gaetano, Guido, Salvatore and Dino.
We came at last into the smell of wine
and cooking in the air, and the band stopped;
the crowd broke, with a splashing noise, and flags,
shot streamers, colored paper, rained on us,
and suddenly, up front, the old square shone
like a sheet of beaten gold in the noon light.

A young man, like a soldier on report,
raced up to Father Ferdinand, and shouldered
his post with a quick circus-skill that pleased
the elders gathered on the churchyard steps.
The priest walked out, and raised his hands. Shouts
    back
told him we owned our God that day, at least,
and with a smile he signalled to the women
waiting along the ropes, as at a race,
and they ran to us with glasses, cups and flagons,
streaming among the ranks where we stood firm,
squat, sweating Samsons, holding up our pride.
When my girl found me, as I knew she would,
her fingers thrusting mint-leaves in my mouth
and holding up the wine-flask for my kiss,
I was the purest penitent standing there,
and I dared the forty Saints to break my back.

The Beaches

I. Flushing Bay

Vlissingen: settled in 1642, chartered in 1645

The water's poisonous: the pretty shine
is a sin. The boat-basin's
a toilet for the borough of Queens, a mirror
for bad dreams. History is wrong
and happened once, what's left is news.

The sun hauls along the piers, stalls
in the out-going tide, slow as a barge,
its colors running in the stinking mud
like blood. My whale of an island's
a dump, snorting through soot and oil.

I must be touched, to look for history
where there's no dignity. I glimpse
beyond the concrete pilings along the shore
towns like clam-shells, in the light's crab tilt
the shade and shimmer of a slum.

Imagine Walt Whitman, old codger, come back to this
flunk shore: solid rhetor, he would spy a gull
so black he'd blink a moment and keep still—
Valley of Ashes, rat-randy acres,
millenial garbage rumbling toward the sea.

Quogue, Patchogue, Montauk, Shinnecock,
are still on the map. What is fame?
See that old Indian looter, Crescent Moon,
easing his canoe past Whitestone Bridge
to trail in tarnished water his silver, his scandalous
    name.

II. Up this seashore in some briars

The people reach by subway or expressway
into the outlying districts
on week-end migrations
and leave in the city
      only the convicts on Riker's Island,
      the guvnmnt.

Gilgo, Moses, Captree, Jones Island,
charter buses dump their bales of children—
special areas marked for touch football,
               red rover,
               capture-the-flag,
all the non-contact sports.
The contact is under the water:
Venus of the chapped hands,
bored and bronzed Apollos, guarding their lives.

Jones Island a short dog-leg to Long Beach:
"America's Healthiest City,"
cabana clubs, mah jong by the pool, outsiders forbidden.

Reckouwacky—*place of our people*—
seven miles of boardwalk free,
the Canarsies, the Montauks are gone,
the Old Age homes are due for a rebirth.

Over the Rockaway inlet
you turn
see the high-rise extinct
parachute insignia,
deserts of beach backed up by slums.
Blow-fish off the pier;
people drinking beer.

Coney is, of course, three subways near.
The trash is pretty much under control.
The blacks and whites do not riot there, though they
    fight.

The pollution of South Beach on Staten Island
is chemically insured;
the sand is smooth as sugar, and free;
there are some mean-spending towns
whose newness accounts for their sparkle.

Wolf's Pond,
the furthest from New York Bay,
is least filthy.
The waters that wash South Beach
are classified B.
(Keep your heads above water.)

The Poetry Group
reads on Gansevoort Pier, next to the city dump:
the prettiest poem
is introduced as
"the waitress from Tony's."
Children run, dodging and giggling,
among the odes and the car-wrecks.
The Statue of Liberty waves.

The Parks Department also runs Orchard Beach
in the Bronx,
at the western end of Long Island.
There is no surfing because there is no surf.

At night
the turnstiles clack like crabs in a parched sea,
the searchlight spouts like Moby Dick.

A Word to Maecenas, in his Park

Above the careful shadows of the town
the moon moves, as discreetly as the dream
this statue, underneath her formal beam
might entertain, and still not lose the frown
some hired artist gave him with his gown
out of a prejudice to make him seem
engrossed in some important, civic theme,
and put him looking stiff, and looking down.

All the expensive silver of that light
goes wasting on our proud and settled tribe
who've long forgotten when the last moon shone
that was not but a symbol of space-flight,
or Beauty, that was not a kind of bribe,
or Statues, dreaming anything but stone.

Lines from a Poet in Residence

Quite through with birth, and almost through with
   dying,
I remember my salty week-ends, clean and wicked,
before the money came, the duty of trying.

It was the illiterature of those poems that took me:
mere carnivores and elegies
that came between jobs or to trick a pretty red-head—
even in the back of a car my Muse was quickened.

I was a liar then, and non-platonic;
with the very best of intentions I lied to myself
most often and most happy,
but today my poems are prayers, not gifts and bribes.

Early or late we each come to learn
the republic has a king;
the rules turn out to be pure logarithm
and not a handy whim to get out of a bind
and set things straight—instead they set things crooked
and I've been hellbent over ever since,
honing my poems and keeping my wife in the kitchen,
and married most of all to a Muse that's frigid
with conscience, commands and career.

Some poems come. I get my pay in prose:
a bank account, a name of sorts, some students
who think I'm the king of the hill when I'm not,
and I keep thinking of some way to get out
to get back to my guts, and the language of my anguish.

On the Vanity of Human Wishes

(After the Tenth Satire of Juvenal)

Search where you will—from Maine to Florida—
observe the antics of grown men at work,
Texas oil-men, New York speculators,
it is the same no matter where you turn:
we study horoscopes and racing-sheets,
seek absolution from our analysts,
or if we court success the classic way
we bet our dollars and our mortgages
on pills, on vitamin-cures, on lotteries.
We make of living one grand traffic-jam
from Washington, D. C., to Disneyland,
and pray for luck and speed, then fall, a prey
to our own gambler's greed. Luck is a lie,
and speed its tricky feet: we get nowhere,
and all that we divine is devastation.
I tell you this, and I'm no fortune-teller.

Where is the soul that is free from pride and error?
We treat truth like a black man in the slums.
We call it peace, but what we have is war,
and a President is destroyed by its grim power.
We say Prosperity but we mean Plague:
the streams and rivers are dying of our wealth,
the garbage glows like bullion under the sun.
We are as impotent as the stranded whale
choked in its fat off the South Asian beach,
mere blubber-and-oil, a freak of history,
to light the lamps of studious generals
lusting for empery. O false ambition!
is there guerilla war in Monte Carlo?
is there a CIA in Liechtenstein?
As tourists we are warned to watch our dollars—
but nobody robs a peasant of his dollars.
At night we walk the streets, hugging our wallet,
as though it were a baby at the breast.

Poverty grins, and whistles in the dark,
and turns its pockets out to show the holes
to any hold-up man who wants to see.
We fear the envy of our starving allies,
for behind the War Lord's back the beggars laugh.

We bribe the pulpit—church or synagogue—
and make meek application (tongue in cheek)
for increase and promotion in man's sight:
do we know the responsibility of riches,
that the gods and goddesses can kill with kindness?
A humble man won't sicken on plain beer:
champagne's the poison, in its crystal cup
that glitters, bright as envy, in our grasp.
Of two old sages, whom shall I commend:
Democritus, who had a sense of humor,
and chuckled every time he stepped outside
and counted the neon-vanities of the town,
or Heraclitus, whose eyes filled with tears?
Laughter is cheap enough: I marvel at
the store of tears that Heraclitus drew from.
Democritus, he almost died of laughing,
yet in his day there were no parking-lots,
no generals as college-chancellors,
no draft, no Swedish films, and not one moon-shot.

What if he'd seen our Mayor on his Honda,
leading the parade to the town's new pool,
dressed like a Nazi—black and beautiful—
and wearing his helmet like an astronaut?
And what about the band-wagon behind him:
hangers-on, ward-heelers, and the Ward Boss
propped like a mummy in his limousine?
Above us stalked the eagle on the flag;
(for all that, we were sprayed with pigeon-shit.)
Then came the Mothers, trailing their white crepe,
the children, like tame robots in their stalls,
the local church contingents, the brass band,
the pensioners, the quiet, well-dressed Negroes—
he is their creditor, they are his friends.

His mind poised, like a finger to the wind,
Democritus would have laughed, a real holiday:
small men with long cigars are comical;
in swallow-tails we all of us look like penguins.
He was a country boy, and solid proof
not every hick's a hick. How he'd have laughed—
trouble or trick just one big titillation,
man's tears and joys the same. And as for Lady Luck,
he would have snapped his fingers, told her to "Get lost!"

The Statue of Liberty herself must laugh
at our petitions: favors by the ton.
You pin your dollars to the saint's long robe
or put a plaque up in the rectory,
it's all the same—Fame, the millstone, drags
the great man down. Fame's perquisite is envy,
and he is shackled in a junk of medals.
The climate changes: down his statue comes;
at the city warehouse his furniture is auctioned.
Where's Sherman Adams now, or Bobby Baker?
Nailed to the News. Who are good fellows now?
They're made the butt of a reporter's quip,
the theme of sermons, punch-lines for a comic
a single season; then they die away
like dead leaves gathered on a compost-heap.
Today you get up early, scoot to town,
and jostle with the crowd for a clear seat:
the court-room spectacle is Jimmy Hoffa,
a bull in handcuffs, led to sacrifice—
". . . that little tub of lard!" ". . . but they're all crooks!"
"It's no surprise to me!" "Who turned him in?"
"Who turned state's evidence . . .?" "Who's getting off?"
A House Committee called him in: *routine.*
The Law's routine's a vaudeville routine.

And what about our *populus romanus?*
It follows headlines, as it always has,
and votes for scandal; and if Lady Luck
had hauled him up instead of dragged him down
it would be cheering him, not jeering him.

Such is celebrity, the gambler's game,
and now that we're a Great Society
our ballots are not worth bribing—citizens
who once struck for the forty-hour week,
the union-shop, who balked the Fascist horde,
spend their rewards now on cheap racing cars;
the American Dream is—a long, paid vacation.
Would you be famous, great, as Hoffa is,
and draw his salary? Reward your aides
with station-wagons, country cottages?
Be guest at banquets for the Governor,
attend a conference at the White House too?

Why not? Think of the pretty go-go girls,
the body-guards, the soft, expensive clothes,
the week-ends in Miami in the winter.
Why not? You needn't wish to rape and pillage
to have that kind of power over life.
But in the grand game that you would be playing,
how many millions worth of fame is worth
the headlong doom that goes along with it?
And would you like now to share Hoffa's cell?
Which would you rather own, Dodd's senate seat,
or the town-stamp at Podunk or Dogpatch,
a Justice of the Peace for traffic fines?
Remember Crassus; better, think of Pompey,
that noble tower looming over Rome,
a veritable mountain-climber of a man
to whom the Alps of fame were women's breasts,
for he sought fame as other men seek Thais.
He lost his head all right; the gods made sure.
There are few kings who live to die in bed;
most get to Hades with holes in their heads.

Our children go to Sunday school, and learn
of famous men (but not how Fame undid them)—
those *servants of mankind*, where are they now?
His very dedication to the peace
struck Gandhi down, who would not raise a hand.

As for that blacksmith's son, born of rude folk,
who dreamed his father's dream of the common man
and clawed his way to power crying *Rome!*,
he finished on a hook, like a pig's haunch,
derided by the mob. Unfriendly gods!
the boon they grant is as touchy as an asp.

And so it is we merit our reward,
and earn our stripes, our buttons brass and gold,
our medal's ticket to eternity.
The Purple Heart will buy a purple robe
and lead the State, for mankind dotes upon
the wounded veteran who heals us all.
Ah, Notoriety! What is your gift?
The game's beyond us but we play the game.

The well-known congressman, the bold D. A.,
how often has he broken mothers' hearts
to win convictions, send his tumbrils-ful
of prisoners to jail? He makes his mark
and gains new office; with the victory
forgets his old ideals—the War on Crime—
and sits to dinner with a gangster-chief.
Or General MacArthur, think of him,
for whom the crown of Asia was too small.
Called back to his own land, he played the game
of President, despite the President.
Surrounded by old men and foolish youths,
the agèd darling of the Gold Star Mothers,
he bore his grudge like Cato, stiff and straight,
sent news releases from his hotel suite
and dreamed of conquest. Poor old Hannibal,
to waste your lion's dotage on coyotes!
He lost that last campaign, a warrior
whose final victory was shame and silence.
What shall we tell our schoolboys of MacArthur?
Remember well the story of Alexander
who had not worlds enough; he's in his cage
of rubble now, the dandelion's slave,
and keeps his court with Xerxes, and the stones.

We pray, we plot, we dream of a long life;
we make of medicine a time-machine:
a hair-dye will not keep the years away.
Observe that face, as smooth as margarine,
beneath the henna-rinse: she dares not chew
except in nibbles, lest her teeth fall out,
and when she talks she whispers. Her weak voice
is hoarse with age, and like a locust's rasp.
Not all the Floridas in the galaxy
will smooth those wrinkled cheeks, now camouflaged
behind expensive creams. We would live long,
yet only youth has true variety:
the old all look alike, like grasshoppers,
shrill voices, trembling hands, bald heads, sharp knees,
and a terror over food—sighs and complaints.
They are a burden to their families,
and even the fortune-hunter turns from them.
For them the hope of sex is of a gland
as shriveled as a raisin, or a flag
that's at half-mast to stay, sad holiday.
What other senses do they have to lose?
They must find joy in watching music sung
for they cannot hear the diva, the sweet harp;
they crouch in theaters, hands up to their ears,
and tire their friends, who spend the whole night
    shouting.
Their only hobbies now are aches and pains;
diseases dance around them in a band.
They have more troubles than Venus had lovers
and are encyclopaedias of plague:
one has arthritis, or a hernia,
another one a cataract, a third
has hardened arteries, or half a brain.
Who'd be a bed-case hated by his nurse?
The profit of long life is loss of love;
you bury sons, you're quit of all your friends.
Live long then, and keep chattering to the shadows:
Tithonus, you'll recall, cried for an end.

There's still another side to all of this;
now let the young ones listen for awhile.
Though mothers pray for lovely sons and daughters,
a lad as handsome as John Barrymore,
a daughter prettier than poor Marilyn,
think how one lived and how the other died.
Such beauty in this world is always fated:
the imperious girl who has no need of brains
will learn, and soon enough, that beauty breaks
as dolls break. There are always other dolls.
What father wants a beautiful son? a clown
who lives off women, only sweats in bed,
and lives a puppet's life, a woman's toy?
Dolls! Toys! Plain girls need no pimps
to find their work for them. Unlovely boys
do all their plowing where it counts, outside
in nature's fields, and will not lack for bread.
Go to it then, proud parents, precious brats.
You'll say to me, "Why not? Latona preened
herself on her Diana's beauty." Yes!
And how about the story of Lucretia?
A rapist's midnight miracle was she,
who was so beautiful she killed herself.
As for that dainty son of yours, reflect
on Nero's preference for such a type;
he never gamboled with cripples, that's for sure,
or buggered after some clumsy, skinny lad.
Your sweet Endymion will die a son
but not a husband. Let it worry you.

"Shall men then pray for nothing?" Who's to say?
I'd leave it to the gods the good we get,
and what's right in a world we never made;
they know us better than we know ourselves
and deal with us according to our natures.
With us, desire traps. What we call hope
is but a nervous buzzing in the head.
We ask for wife and off-spring; the gods know
the kind we'll get—the kind that we deserve.

Yet if a man would pray, and sacrifice,
and drop his money in the wicker plate,
then let sound mind in a sound body be
the miracle he asks for, and a heart
that's strong enough to die, and eyes to see
our days for what they are, mere butterflies
that feed a moment on a morning's gold.
Let him expect no future but hard work;
let him be calm, and curb his appetite.
Let him compete in toil with Hercules,
not dream of junketing like King Farouk.
What I am saying you already know:
it is ourselves that we must truly seek;
we are our own real worth and way to peace.
For want of wit we make of Lady Luck
a sleazy goddess of cheap dreams. The truth
is not so fickle nor so far from home—
we make our luck ourselves, the darling and the doom.

Spoiled by all my Tyrants

Spoiled by all my tyrants, and whomped to bed,
but kissed for my blond curls from time to time,
then shoved to school as if I were the ewe
the principal had asked for, all my brothers
gruff and soon gone growing, to come back
and bring me all the grace of the Green Fair,
I had a precious training, and clean hands.
On the cold bench my mother creaked her grief
to understand my words: the school salute
I pressed upon the flag could only scare her.
O my dark kind, why have you left me bleating,
to learn trite courtesies and lowland ways,
when all I wanted was my rightful place
as the last son, beside my father's table?
Tell him that as I grow, my hair turns darker.

A City by the Sea

(for Selma, after shopping for her)

Houses, lopped by shadow: glinting blocks
of color scattered in the light-and-dark
abrasions of the sun: horns: children's noise
out of an alley, kick-the-can: the poise
of a policeman, sauntering: the stark
brick chunk of a church whose four-square clocks

toll me a heaven of cast-iron bells:
smells: coffee, cooking grease, damps on concrete,
and from the junkyard, rubber on a fire:
over the wind, gulls, screaming headlines: higher,
a neon bird, wing-spread above the street,
pecking electric grain, while the pattern swells

in purgatorian inventory: a dog,
a red-faced merchant, toddling pensioners
at their slow walk across the busy town,
lads to hand-wagons, housewife in a frown
poking at silks on stalls: the tricky jeers
of sparrows in the gutter: like a frog

some hackie croaking gossip by his stand
to a news-vendor: this is where we live,
in four tight rooms, me, my sweet, tired girl.
I'd be your lute-player, my lovely girl,
in a meadow in Provence, but here men give
the meadow boxed in bits, at the fruit-stand—

apples, like baubles shining under glass:
the small, round worlds of oranges: the green-
barbed riot of the shaggy escarolle:
bananas, decorous upon the pole,
in abstract dream: the mother-of-pearl sheen
of onion, rainbow-eye, from where I pass

to the soft-scented fennel, taste for free
its cooling water-words that bless the store
where fig-rows dangle, truffles, sugar-cane.
(I think now there should leap upon the scene
some wilder keeper than old Joe, and roar,
a pirate with a cutlass after me

for trespassing inside his treasure-trove.)
Aspect of the large soul our city has,
revealing us in all our gross, true taste,
(the spirit dwindles if the belly waste!)
I gaze about me, princely in my ease,
and reap the weather's ransom for my love.

As on a "human sea" then, Love, I swim,
borne forward by my love for what is real
to you, more real than poem or Provence.
Take from my hand this happy happenstance
of herbs and garlands from a ramshackle vale,
the green and gay plucked from the gray and grim.

Bruce Woodford

Preferences

I like a verse like broken glass
purpled in suns over a barbed land
that makes you bleed

I like a poem like a wary foot
poised in a pause of walking
in a place of snakes

I like a song like whetted wind
edged on a shrill feather
truer than arrows

I like an end like a thorned winter
white on a tree full of needles
aimed every direction

Thighbone

Around you once, flesh wove a vine of fire,
And passion pressed its dark arterial wine
To wake in you the Saturnalia, Desire,
And yield possession to the libertine.

But now undone and fathomed once, here, both
The fruitless bones and vineyard frames recline
In tired disuse, where only winds unclothe
And a morning glory curves its flowered vine.

Escapade

I saw colonnades of Babylon,
And vineyards filled with grape;
Last night I saw them trampled down
At the scene of Pluto's rape.

I saw a face without a face
Laughing in an empty street
Where the Victory of Samothrace
Perused her stony feet.

I drank from waters of a bloody sea,
Fell drunk on red Sahara sand;
Woke to find Gethsemane
Covered by my broken hand . . .

I dreamed I walked the ends of earth
Then came stampeding back;
I set me down in child mirth
To pluck star-petals from the zodiac.

Halloween

Calling through a dark time door to door,
my visit taps its cane. Yet nothing opens.
Though breath beat hard on panels tough as air,
no dog nor master of the house replies.

And nowhere I taste more panic than when I hear
the sudden cricket leap up hollows of my wrist.
A wind licks loud as grass about my feet
and bending pavement listens at my listening.

Something near (the blind eye knows like memory)
down marrowed alley and tenement of bone
maps each nightly step that follows me,
tunes the tendon at my heel,

                     and though I run,
shall one night quickly put the blade between
my lean ribs long before the heart gets home.

The Beach Party

It all began with kissing, of course;
then the straps came down,
and I touched each soft nippled moon
as the tide started in; and the trunks came off . . .
And the hair, O the smell of her hair
was sea-weed rich and tangled and fire to the touch.
And naked then after our long swim
under the tall tugging light that moves waves
and traces veins of cold fire in the foam,
we lay late on the shore making love,

leg-tangled and thigh, into the pre-dawn dark—
the bonfire we built had burned itself down,
the crowd had gone home, and beer had run out.
Only the sand beneath us was warm
and itched with the scratch of our love
pounding its print to the distant pulse of a surf
where the sea-lion slipped back deep
into its sea-lion cave.

O surely the world must have begun
on the seaweed edge in the soft dimpled sand
under the light of moon's tugging
surely love was the first act
after we walked from the wave onto the high continent
and the first blind living spurt of that tide started in.

April

April, and the nippling river
swells with rain; the air goes green
again around its trees, tight-grained
in this seasoned wind.
                              Grass flutes a fever
shrill as throats in feather;
                              each sly touch
of water wakes with a mossy itch.
Skin sweetens.
                  And tiny hooves dance goats.

For you

Storm opened with a green sky
air whispered and a smell of rain
sang like sound in the sudden on-
set of leaves
                    coming down coming
down   sharp with thunder
                                   I waited
under a green-tall roof under
a shouting tree where a wind
scattered the children like voices
coming into the house
                         and far
far off thunder
                    like an old man
stumbling his fill of whiskey home
under the tall shouting tree
I waited
            for you and wind
and the voices of children
                              caught
in the crack of light coming down
like skipping stone
                      out of a sound
of sky opening to the green
of storm   of storm
                      like a tree
growing full of its rain   like leaves
over me
            and wind and a roof
where I waited
                    for you

Moth

Coming back
          in a dark
over a long road
               to another city
was a long time ago
                    now
but
   I kept coming back
past
   barbwire
               and broken sheds
in white fields
of a winter night

               And that was all
long ago
          I kept coming back
the road running under
me
   from my lights
toward another time
and lights
          of another city

And I kept coming
                    back to it
circling in from a dark
like a hill
          descending
down
   to the lighted
                    city

and O
     the one I kept
always coming back to

til I was crisp
as this paper

Abstract I: Nuns on a Grey Landscape

Grey Nuns
Crossing the grey dunes
Following their anonymous path
From cloister to chapel's weathered walls;
And between sharp swords of encroaching sedge
Wind-singing answer to each Lover's prayer,
Between their Aves and the wild gull-shriek
From living air wings strange antiphony
Drawing both beyond toward a Timeless Sea.

Has your ear learned that sea-song, sweet sister
Like a child become, holding the heart's shell
From earth's hollow shore?
Caught in the pearled vortex of a mystery
Where no wave dies, has flesh become Love's conch
Sounding a tideless sea?
What Word, held inwardly, do your lips express
Empty and unknown to one who only hears
Wind humming in dry grass?

Is it blood's slow beat, drop by drop
Suffered to Love's yet living thorn,
That drains all color from your solemn face?
And is that Phoenix somewhere still reborn
Out of the sacred fire where Love's first dance
Consumed itself into your ashen Grace?

Grey Nuns
On a grey landscape
Crossing dunes by a perpetual sea—
No voice cries out that is heard
When winds die over the sand's sift;
Only the sisters counting in low monotone their beads,
Sweet faces withdrawn into grey hoods
Toward a sea-surf's other sounding
On shores where no wild gulls fly.

From The Adobe Makers

Invocation

While rainfall sounds softly
and night covers the vigas of heaven,
lie still my love.
Let us enter the kingdom of the corn tassel
and the melon's Eden.
Let the hunter take his deer:
the wound lie open to receive its arrow;
and rooted wand reach river.

Let me come into your eye.

Let the spent seed fall into its water circle,
blessing each breath born of the sweet mouth
where spirit walks and all song
makes image.

Let naked dark slope over the soft heaven
and rain fall softly
deep into the naked earth.
Let the storm be swift
and gentle.

Lie still my love.
Let me come into your eye.

Let us make gods
from the breathless silence
deep
at the storm's center.

—fragment

One church night's ten o'clock tolled its people
altarward   old women in rebozos   men
wrenched overalled from work their hand-earned sweat
still marinating callouses   feet   boot-wearied
and tavern still upon their breath
                                   Our gas-stop
pumped some wrong moment from a boy impatient
to be gone   fill our tank and drift with the town
settling night dust out of its arclights   follow
its sounding wether into the dark
                                   Street emptied
whatever curfew or occasion gathered
dimmed light and closed its doors

                              Fifty miles farther
in our dark we still remembered   bells   old adobe
and that echoed sibilance of quickened feet

Running the Tide

And then names
                the names that held a road intact
small halts and hesitations from a questing dream
San Luis—
          Garcia—
                  Costilla—
                           Questa—
                                   Threading the line
we ran our tar-dark span of highway   gut-spun
from a spidering past—web-frail and warp
in a time mazed weave beyond our own breath brief
ravel of remembering—   *Far*
                        west from here a point where
                        you stand four corners deep
                        in the true wind's direction
                        and compassed center of
                        the heart's aimed arrow

                              South
                                    south now down
our own sun-blind meridian—following . . .

        where   north once they came out of the sun
and by no map but the unchartered seasons
chased each shadowed contour of their dream past
waking   wherever day by ridge or river
led to nights of sleeping toward no certain star
—til fanged bush and drift of sand ground eyes out
teeth from wind-weathered jaws   and filled the cages
of their breath
                              South
through little towns beading our map-line bleak
as desperate prayers in that starve of winter—
brown villages where snow-bound hands hoard fire
from pine-quick hearths and cold breaks smoke off thin
as its chimney moan   the wind-dogs harried us

And we ran
        all valley long
                        —sun sky
                        four directions
                        wind and
                        a wide land—
                                    down to Questa

                              *

—snow-fold and fence
webbed field
            blue shadow's burn
and barbed blaze of ice-
fractured sun
            in the skied
winter's turn—

We sharpened in a whet of wind—
                        Trim ship   I said
Rough still ahead   said Jim   Twenty gravel miles
yet by map   —and rode that relicked land out keen
edged as its air

        I watched cold distance take us
like a running tide whipped to a white surf   yet
always our eyes' margins kept that broken thrust
of mountains   believing always over each
coming crest around some next turning past one
pined ridge more a cold road must lead us somewhere
warming to a certainty
                           And if I walked
I thought . . .
        Time hammered in its stone   bald
sky made miniature my ghost-nagged memory
dream even   shrank like dying water   blood cooled
and some hush of the wind called   let go . . .
                                 let go . . .

      Sixty million made an infant year
of silence into mountains— *And if I walked*
I thought . . .
             how many miles   *how far . . .*
                           past Questa
to Santa Fe

                       *

        All on the surface now snowed
smooth from plow-stammered furrow to the ditched
trap of our road . . .
            We shipped south in our bones—
Over the white   one black wire tussled the wind
broken loose from its anchoring post   stabbed air
like a fingering tendril in need of spring
mending
        With the cold season riding its fence
pole to pole each chattering strand telegraphed
messages
          older than ice
               Yet everything north
of the face lay in shadow still as a mask—

Far behind
              Sierra Blanca
                        the San Juans . . .
and we came over the valley shoulder shawled
with its winter down to the ice-fringed river—
through Questa dog lean as its mud streets across
the bridged Red in full season flood and beyond
climbed again into seried and pine laced hill
beneath the stone blade cordilleras . . .
                                    Rough still
ahead   said Jim—
                        And one blind bend past slammed us
into that jar-tooth slough and spung of gravel—
twenty mapped-out miles in a skid of hyphens
(and so map right by damn as someone's spit wet
thumb shoved up the wind—*right yes*
                                but less than true. . .)
        —We pitched off high center into the trough
and coasting the rollers took those long land swells
head on under our wheels   Sun tilted and yawed
with each curve in the road   Pine spiked the shroud knot
of cold   but snow held   tight as a sheath
                                        We passed

        Embargo—
              San Cristobal—
                        Arroyo Hondo
                                —paused
in the fume and chime of gas   to stretch for breath
and stamp those dizzy wheels still out of our feet
And if I walked I thought . . .
                        Far off   the reefed peaks
boomed their windy rant   remote as the white break
of a ten mile surf

          How long   I asked   till Taos
The gas pump shrugged   Cold enough and a wind
                          tailing
seven maybe eight miles by crow   (*o how far* . . . How
many stations more to   Santa Fe)
                     Climbing
from the Arroyo then   wind-tailing it past
the pine-spike hills we followed the asphalt crow
—always those sunlight mountains weighing at our
left shoulder   the Sangre de Cristo leaning . . .

               * * *

A Suit of Four was set in Melior, a modern Roman typeface chosen for its sense of forthright originality and solidity. The typesetting was done by Computer Typesetting Company of Louisville, Kentucky. The printing by offset lithography and the perfect binding were by Haywood Publishing Company, Lafayette, Indiana. The text paper is 70-pound Wausau Text with a laid finish, and Mead Mark I is the 100-pound coated cover stock. Design and artwork were by Donald K. Carter, Purdue University graphic designer, and editorial and production supervision were by Diane Dubiel, assistant university editor at Purdue.